A+ books

Nature Starts

Which SEED Is This?

by Lisa J. Amstutz

CAPSTONE PRESS
a capstone imprint

A+ Books are published by Capstone Press,
1710 Roe Crest Drive, North Mankato, Minnesota 56003.
www.capstonepub.com

Library of Congress Cataloging-in-Publication Data
Amstutz, Lisa J.
  Which seed is this? / by Lisa J. Amstutz.
    p. cm.—(A+ Books. Nature starts)
  Includes bibliographical references.
  Summary: "Simple text and full-color photos ask multiple-choice questions about which
plants seeds grow into"—Provided by publisher.
  ISBN 978-1-4296-7552-9 (library binding) – ISBN 978-1-4296-7851-3 (paperback)
  1. Seeds—Juvenile literature. 2. Germination—Juvenile literature. I. Title. II. Series.
QK661.A67 2012
575.6'8–dc23   2011027264

Credits
Katy Kudela, editor; Juliette Peters, designer; Marcie Spence and Svetlana Zhurkin,
    media researchers; Laura Manthe, production specialist

A special thanks to Debbie Folkerts, PhD, Department of Biological Sciences,
    Auburn University, Alabama, for her time and expertise on this project.

Photo Credits
Alamy: Bob Gibbons, 24, Makoto Honda, 22; Ardea: John Mason, 26; Capstone Studio: Karon Dubke,
15 (bottom left and right), 20, 28 (bottom right); Dreamstime: Per Christensen, 23 (bottom right), 29
(bottom left); Shutterstock: 2009fotofriends, 17 (top right), Agita Leimane, 15 (top left), Alessandro
Zocc, 16, 23 (bottom left), almond, 9 (top right), Andrew Orlemann, 27 (bottom left), Anne Kitzman,
7 (top right), 28 (top left), Better Stock, 27 (bottom right), Clarence S. Lewis, 11 (top right), Copit, 13
(top right), Danicek, 14, Dmitriy Yakovlev, 27 (top left), Dream79, 10, duoduo, 23 (top left), Dusan
Zidar, 9 (bottom left), E.O., 7 (bottom right), Elena Stwolovsky, 25 (top left), 29 (bottom middle), Feng
Yu, cover (top right), 19 (bottom right), foto76, 9 (bottom right), Fotokostic, 21 (bottom left), 29 (top right),
FotoYakov, 7 (top left), Galyna Andrushko, cover (middle right), 19 (top left), holbox, 15 (top right), Igor
Borodin, 21 (top right), Igor Murtazin, 21 (top left), Inacio Pires, 11 (bottom right), JetKat, cover (left), 18,
Jozsef Szasz-Fabian, 11 (bottom left), Keysurfing, 17 (bottom left), LianeM, 12, Loskutnikov, 1, 8, Melinda
Fawver, 17 (top left), 29 (top left), Menna, cover (middle right), 19 (top right), 29 (top middle), mimo, 13
(bottom right), 28 (bottom middle), OlegD, 3, Orhan Cam, 13 (top left), pepmiba, 5 (left), pmphoto, 27
(top right), 29 (bottom right), SeDmi, 5 (right), shutswis, 6, silver-john, 21 (bottom right), Smart-foto, 7
(bottom left), Smileus, 4, sunxin, 9 (top left), 28 (top right), Tim Mainiero, 25 (bottom right), tomtsya, 25
(bottom left), Tristan Tan, 11 (top left), 28 (bottom left), Vaaka, cover (bottom right), 19 (bottom left),
Vasilius, 30, Wendy Sue Gilman, 25 (top right), yanuz, 13 (bottom left); Svetlana Zhurkin, 17 (bottom right),
23 (top right)

Note to Parents, Teachers, and Librarians
This Nature Starts book uses full color photographs and a nonfiction format to introduce the
concept of plant life cycles. *Which Seed Is This?* is designed to be read aloud to a pre-reader
or to be read independently by an early reader. Photographs help listeners and early readers
understand the text and concepts discussed. The book encourages further learning by including
the following sections: Glossary, Read More, and Internet Sites. Early readers may need assistance
using these features.

Printed in the United States   5619

THE AMAZING SEED

A seed is the beginning of a new plant. Wind, water, or animals carry a seed to a new spot. There it rests awhile. With the right amount of water and heat, it will sprout.

Often hiding in pulp, a seed has three parts. If you break it open, you will see a tiny plant. Around the plant is food to help it grow. A seed coat on the outside keeps it safe.

Each plant makes its own kind of seeds. These seeds come in many colors, shapes, and sizes.

Can you guess which plant makes each seed?

Keep reading and make your best guess! You can find the correct answers on pages 28 and 29.

These yellow kernels grew in neat rows on a cob before they were removed. The cob grows on the tall stalk of a kind of grass. It is one of the most common plants in the world.

WHICH SEEDS ARE THESE?

WHEAT

CORN

BEAN

OAT

Hint !

You can cook and eat these seeds. People also make cereal, soda, and fuel from them.

The plant that grows from this seed can be 10 feet (3 meters) tall. Its huge flower head is the size of a dinner plate. Both birds and people like to eat these seeds.

WHICH SEEDS ARE THESE?

SUNFLOWER

ROSE

BEAN

WATER LILY

Hint! This plant gets its name from the way it turns to face the sun.

9

The biggest seed in the world grows at the top of a tall tree. This seed weighs up to 50 pounds (23 kilograms). If you crack open the shell, you will find white "meat" and "milk."

WHICH SEED IS THIS?

COCONUT

PINEAPPLE

WALNUT

ORANGE

 Hint

The fruit of this seed helps it to float.
It can cross oceans, washing up on a
faraway beach to sprout and grow.

II

Squirrels often bury these seeds to eat later. Sometimes they forget to dig them up, and the seeds sprout into new trees. These trees can live for hundreds of years.

WHICH SEEDS ARE THESE?

DATE PALM

COFFEE

PEACH

OAK

Hint

Blue jays and deer eat these bitter seeds.
American Indians soaked the seeds in
water to make them taste less bitter.

13

If you cut this fruit around the middle, you will find a star with five points. The star holds five to 10 teardrop-shaped seeds. If you plant a seed, it will grow into a new tree.

WHICH SEEDS ARE THESE?

BANANA

ORANGE

APPLE

GRAPE

 Hint !

You don't eat these seeds, but the fruit makes a yummy snack. You can cook the fruit to make sauce, juice, and pie.

15

These seeds have fruits that whirl and twirl to the ground in spring. Some people call them "helicopters." Each seed will sprout a tree with five-pointed leaves that change colors in fall.

WHICH SEEDS ARE THESE?

MAPLE

CHERRY

SUGARCANE

PINE

Hint! People make sweet syrup from this tree's sap. To make one gallon of syrup, it takes up to 40 gallons (151 liters) of sap.

Each one of these seeds has a bit of fluffy fruit attached. Whoosh! A gust of wind blows the fruit off their stems. Maybe you like to blow on them too. These seeds grow plants with bright yellow flowers.

WHICH SEED IS THIS?

PUSSY WILLOW

DANDELION

DAISY

DAFFODIL

 Hint !

Most people think of these plants as weeds in
their lawn. But long ago, settlers planted them
for food. Their leaves make a tasty salad.

The red, juicy flesh of this fruit hides many small seeds. Long ago, people were afraid to eat this fruit. They thought it was poisonous. Today we make pizza sauce and ketchup from it.

WHICH SEEDS ARE THESE?

WATERMELON

STRAWBERRY

TOMATO

PEPPER

Hint ❗ Most people think of this plant as a vegetable. But scientists call it a fruit. This type of fruit is a berry.

This shiny black seed comes from a meat-eating plant. When an insect touches special hairs on its leaves, the leaves snap shut. The insect is trapped inside. The plant makes special juices to digest it.

WHICH SEED IS THIS?

THISTLE

CACTUS

PITCHER PLANT

VENUS FLYTRAP

 Hint!

This plant grows in North and South Carolina. It grows in bogs, where the soil is poor.

Little hooks make these fruits prickly. They hitch a ride on your sock when you walk through a field. That's how they get to new places to grow. The new plants will have big, hairy leaves that are shaped like hearts.

WHICH SEEDS ARE THESE?

BURDOCK

ROSE

RASPBERRY

POISON IVY

Hint

Did you ever have shoes with Velcro strips instead of shoelaces? The man who invented Velcro got the idea from these seeds.

These seeds start out small. But they grow into the world's tallest trees. Look up to the sky! Each tree has sharp, pointed leaves called needles.

WHICH SEEDS ARE THESE?

EUCALYPTUS

REDWOOD

PINE

BAMBOO

Hint!

These giant trees live a long life! One of these trees can live more than 2,000 years.

Guess What?

How many seeds did you name? Check out the answer key to find out if your answers were correct.

PAGES 6-7

Did you guess these seeds correctly? They are from a **CORN** plant. Maize is another name for corn. People first grew corn in Mexico.

PAGES 8-9

SUNFLOWER seeds make a good snack for birds and people. Sunflowers are easy plants to care for. These seeds just need a sunny spot to grow.

PAGES 10-11

If planted, this giant seed will grow a **COCONUT PALM**. These trees grow in places where it is warm all year.

PAGES 12-13

A small acorn grows into a mighty **OAK** tree. There are several hundred kinds of oak trees.

PAGES 14-15

Crunch! Take a bite from an **APPLE** and you'll find these tiny seeds. If planted, these seeds will grow into apple trees. But it takes four to eight years before a tree is ready to grow apples.

MAPLE seeds get the name "helicopter" from their flat, thin wings. A gust of wind blows these seeds far.

This seed with fluffy fruit belongs to a **DANDELION**. This plant's name means "lion's tooth." The edges of its leaves look like teeth.

Did you guess that these seeds are from a **TOMATO**? Most tomatoes are red. But tomatoes can be orange, yellow, pink, or white.

This tiny seed grows into a **VENUS FLYTRAP**. This meat-eating plant catches flies, spiders, and crickets. A flytrap takes five to 12 days to finish its meal.

These prickly burs come from a **BURDOCK** plant. Sticky burs catch on animals' fur and people's clothing. Removing the burs drops the seeds in new places.

Packed inside a cone, these tiny seeds come from a **REDWOOD** tree. Giant redwoods grow mainly in California.

29

Seeds are everywhere! They grow flowers and trees. They make fruits and vegetables. To get a seed to sprout, put it in some dirt. Give the seed sunshine and water. It takes time, but you might grow a tree, vegetable, or flower.

Glossary

berry—a soft, round fruit that grows on bushes or plants; berries have many seeds inside of them

bog—an area of wet, spongy land

cob—the center part of an ear of corn on which the kernels grow

cone—the hard, woody seed-holding part of a redwood tree

digest—to break down for food

fruit—the part of a plant that contains seeds; some fruits are fleshy or juicy and can be eaten

kernel—a grain or seed of corn

poisonous—able to harm or kill with poison or venom

pulp—the soft juicy or fleshy part of a fruit or vegetable

sap—a fluid found inside plants and trees

seed coat—the outer layer of a seed

sprout—to start to grow

stem—the part of a plant that connects the roots to the leaves

weed—a plant that grows where it is not wanted

Read More

Aston, Dianna Hutts. *A Seed Is Sleepy.* San Francisco: Chronicle Books, 2007.

McElroy, Jean. *It's Harvest Time!* New York: Little Simon, 2010.

Wade, Mary Dodson. *Seeds Sprout!* I Like Plants! Berkeley Heights, N.J.: Enslow Pub., 2009.

Internet Sites

FactHound offers a safe, fun way to find Internet sites related to this book. All of the sites on FactHound have been researched by our staff.

Here's all you do:

Visit *www.facthound.com*

Type in this code: 9781429675529

Check out projects, games and lots more at
www.capstonekids.com

32